Hindu Spirituality
In A Nutshell

by *Nilesh Parab*

Copyright © 2005 by Nilesh Parab.

All rights reserved. No part of this work may be reproduced or transmitted in any form or by any means electronic or mechanical, including photocopying, recording, or by any information storage or retrieval system without the prior written permission of the copyright owner.

ISBN: 978-1-4357-5700-4

Table of Contents

Rebirth and the Soul 1
Two Realms of Existence 4
Creation-Annihilation 7
The Trapped Soul 11
Karma: The Puppeteer 16
Liberation/Mukti 22
The Journey Home 26

Hindu Spirituality In A Nutshell

- **Rebirth and the Soul**

When we use the term "I" or "Me" we refer to it as a single, atomic entity. A combination of our body, our intellect, our emotions, our memories, etc.

But in spiritual terms, the meaning of "I" is different. Our single self is divided into different parts:

- The Body, and all the things which come with the body, namely our senses, our intellect, emotions, etc. This Body is the *material component*. It encompasses all the things which die when our body dies.
- The Soul (also called Jiva or Atma). This soul is the *spiritual component*. The part which does not die when we die.

Hindu Spirituality In A Nutshell

The Body is like a house for the Soul. When we die, it is like our soul leaving the old house (old body) and entering into a new one (new body) when we are reborn.

The Soul is eternal. It never dies. It just changes houses.

The Body also houses another entity: Paramatma or God. There is a piece of God in each of us. In this capacity as Paramatma, He is like an observer. Or more like an accountant. Whenever we take any action (good/bad), our Soul (Atma) asks permission from God (Paramatma) and then proceeds to carry out that action. And He just notes down that action in our account/journal. This account of ours, where our deeds are noted down, is our Karma account.

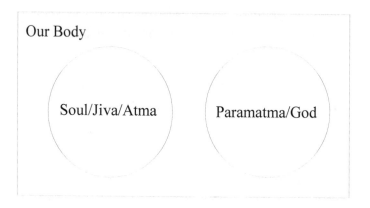

Fig.1

This piece of God (Paramatma) is like our spiritual Siamese twin. He follows the Soul (Atma) everywhere. From birth to birth. From body to body.

Hence, in further discussions, we will merge Atma and Paramatma together and refer to them as the Soul or Jiva.

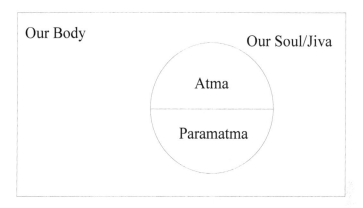

Fig.2

The following illustrations shows the process of death and rebirth, when a soul leaves the old body (which is dead) and enters a new body.

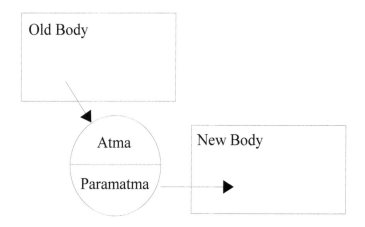

Fig.3

- **Two Realms of Existence**

According to Hindu scriptures, entire existence is divided into two parts:

  - The Material World, which includes everything in nature as we know it, right from the smallest atoms, to the largest mountains, the planets, the stars, the entire cosmos, all galaxies and universes.
  - The Spiritual World, which cannot be seen or felt with our current material senses. This Spiritual World is much, much larger than the Material World.

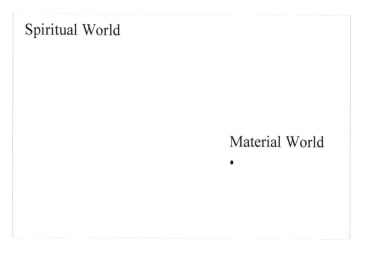

Fig.4

The Material World is comprised of the heavenly planets, earth, and the hellish planets.

Hindu Spirituality In A Nutshell

```
┌─────────────────────────────────────────────┐
│ Spiritual World                             │
│                                             │
│                                             │
│        ┌───────────────────────────────┐    │
│        │  ┌─────────┐                  │    │
│        │  │ Heaven  │   Material World │    │
│        │  └─────────┘                  │    │
│        │        ┌─────────┐            │    │
│        │        │  Earth  │            │    │
│        │        └─────────┘            │    │
│        │              ┌─────────┐      │    │
│        │              │  Hell   │      │    │
│        │              └─────────┘      │    │
│        └───────────────────────────────┘    │
└─────────────────────────────────────────────┘
```

Fig.5

When we die, the Paramatma/God in our Soul assigns us to a new body, according to the actions which we have accumulated in our Karma account.

If we have accumulated good Karma (through good actions) in our Karma account, we will be assigned a body on one of the heavenly planets.

For bad Karma we will be assigned a body on one of the hellish planets.

Even this new body, assigned on either a heavenly planet or a hellish planet, is mortal. It is not like the eternal

Hindu Spirituality In A Nutshell

heaven or the eternal fires of hell, like in other religions.

So, after another lifetime in heaven, we will eventually die. Then the Karma account kicks in again. The Paramatma/God assigns us to yet another body, according to the new Karma we have accumulated in this heavenly birth. Thus, if we have accumulated bad Karma in heaven, then we will be assigned a body back on earth or even to Hell.

In this way, our Soul is caught in the cycle of life and death and rebirth. Changing bodies again and again. Transported between Heaven, Earth, and Hell. Assigned different bodies on these planets on subsequent births.

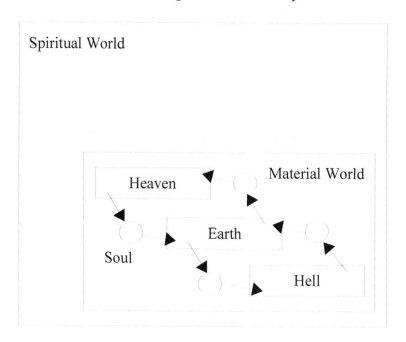

Fig.6

Hindu Spirituality In A Nutshell

- **Creation-Annihilation**

The Material World is annihilated after being in existence for "a thousand ages". Everything in the Material World, all life forms, all non-living entities, all planets, the entire universe gets destroyed at the end of that period.

It then stays destroyed for an equivalent "thousand ages".

After this period of non-existence, it is recreated, with all Souls, all life forms, all non-living entities, all planets, the universe getting recreated. The Karma from their earlier existence is carried forward in this new creation cycle.

So, the Material World is mortal. It dies every "thousand ages", and is reborn after another "thousand ages".

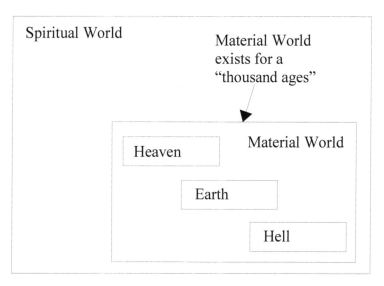

Fig.7

Hindu Spirituality In A Nutshell

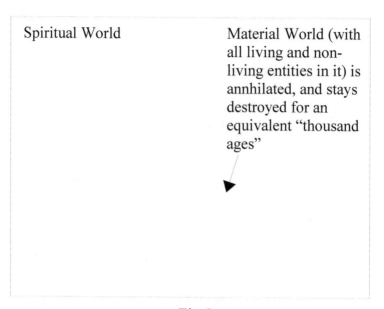

Fig.8

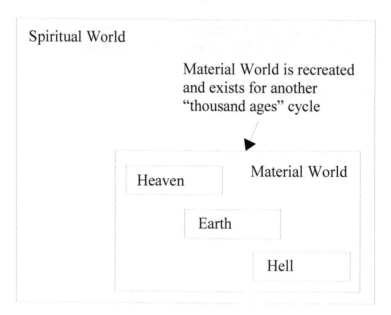

Fig.9

Hindu Spirituality In A Nutshell

In this way, the creation-annihilation cycle of the Material World goes on and on.

The "thousand ages" period corresponds to millions of years. Thus the Material World remains existent for millions of years, and non-existent for millions of years.

In contrast, the Spiritual World is immortal. It is eternal. It does not undergo cyclic creation and annihilation like the Material World does.

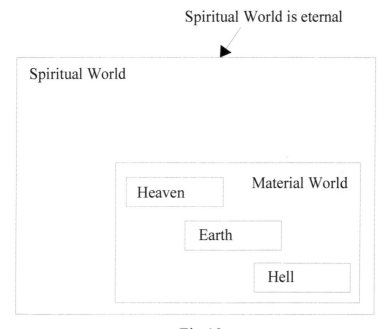

Fig.10

The Spiritual World exists even when the Material World is annihilated.

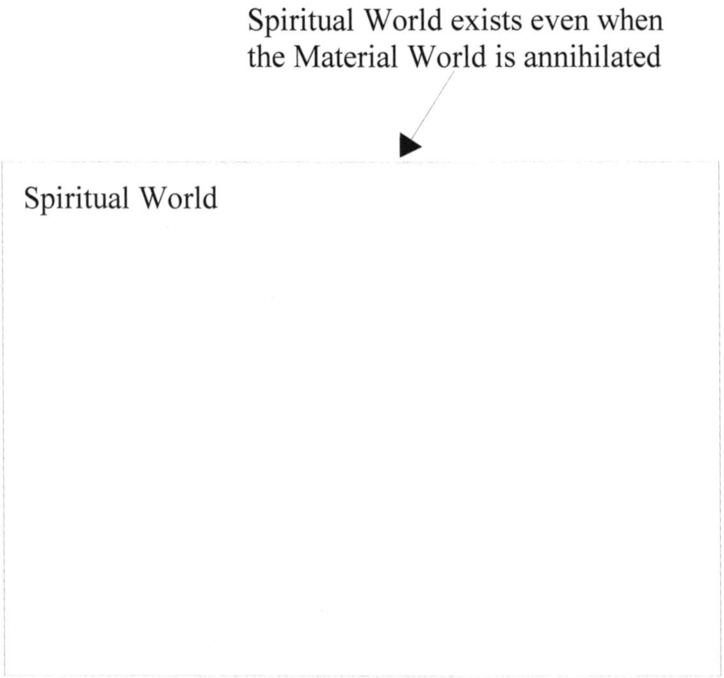

Spiritual World exists even when
the Material World is annihilated

▶

Spiritual World

Fig.11

The creation-annihilation of the Material World is controlled by God, manifested as the Hindu Holy Trinity of:

- Brahma – The Creator of the Material World.
- Vishnu – The Preserver of the Material World.
- Shiva – The Destroyer of the Material World.

When in existence, the Material World is sustained by the female energies of the Hindu Holy Trinity, depicted by:

- Saraswati – The Goddess of Knowledge/Arts.
- Laxmi – The Goddess of Fortune/Beauty.
- Shakti – The Goddess of Power.

Hindu Spirituality In A Nutshell

- **The Trapped Soul**

We have always assumed that our body, our mind, our intellect, our memories define us.

But now we are being told that these do not define who we are. Our bodies (and the associated mind, intellect, memories) are just temporary. They are like houses which we change after living in for some time. They are like clothes which we change after wearing for some time.

So, what *does* define us? What *does* define who we are?

Answer: *The Soul*. That part of us which is eternal. The spiritual part of us, as opposed to the material part of us (our body).

The Soul is the "I" which defines us as spiritual (eternal) entities.

Thus, we have a *spiritual* Soul trapped inside a *material* Body, inside a *Material World*.

See Fig.12 on the next page.

Please note that when we say Material World here, it includes all the heavenly, earth and hellish planets.

Fig.12

For the sake of clarity, we will remove the body rectangle from future diagrams. Thus, we have the following diagram.

Fig.13

Thus, we have a spiritual Soul trapped in the Material World.

Hindu Spirituality In A Nutshell

Everyone, every living entity in this world, is a spiritual being (Soul), trapped in the Material World. Right from the chaste puritan to the worst scoundrel.

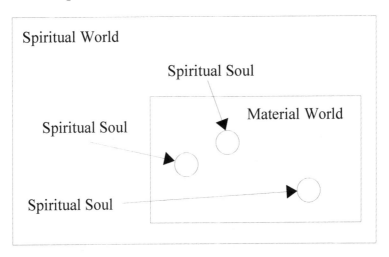

Fig.14

Now, let us sit back for a while and look at the big picture of the Material and Spiritual Worlds.

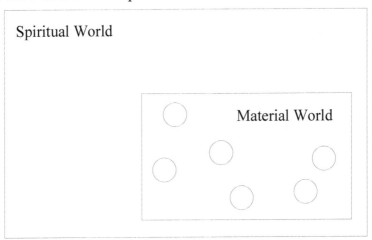

Fig.15

Hindu Spirituality In A Nutshell

So, if the Souls/Jivas are spiritual beings belonging to the Spiritual World, then what are they doing in the Material World??

Answer: The Souls/Jivas are *trapped* in the Material World.

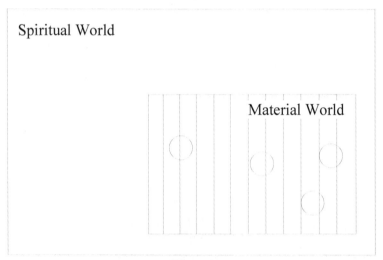

Fig.16

What traps the Souls/Jivas in the Material World? What keeps them from reaching the Spiritual World where they belong?

Answer: The Souls/Jivas in the Material World are *bound* in the Material World due to their Karma accounts (their past deeds and desires).

See Fig. 17 on the next page, which shows how the Souls are trapped in the Material World by their Karma.

Hindu Spirituality In A Nutshell

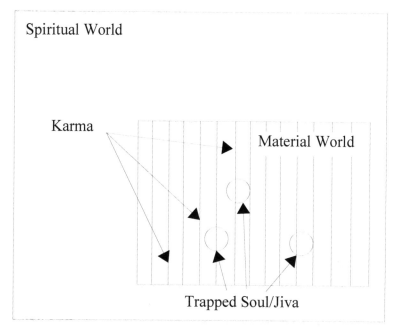

Fig.17

This raises two questions:

- How does Karma trap us in the Material World?
- How does a Soul/Jiva renounce his/her Karma account and become liberated and return to the Spiritual World?

To answer these questions, we have to discuss the nature of Karma in a little detail.

Hindu Spirituality In A Nutshell

- **Karma: The Puppeteer**

A good analogy of Karma is that of a person taking a train ride.

A person takes a train to go downtown. The person is thinking "I am going downtown". But in reality, the person is doing nothing. The *train* is going downtown. The train is doing the work. The train decides where to turn, where not to turn, where to stop, where not to stop, according to the rail tracks, stations and timetable that have been laid out for it. The person just sits back and enjoys the ride.

Similarly, in our life, we think that "I am doing this deed". But, in reality, our Karma is making us do the deed. Our Karma is just like the train. And we (our souls) are just like passengers taking the ride. Our Karma decides what to do, what not to do, where to turn, where not to turn, where to stop, where not to stop, according to the tracks, stations and timetable that has been laid out for our lives. We are just passengers who are following the timetable of Karma.

Just like the train makes the choices according to the rail tracks and timetable laid out, our Karma makes the choices for us according to the path and timetable laid out for our lives. We just think "I am making this choice". But in reality, the choice has already been made according to our Karma timetable.

See Fig. 18 on the next page.

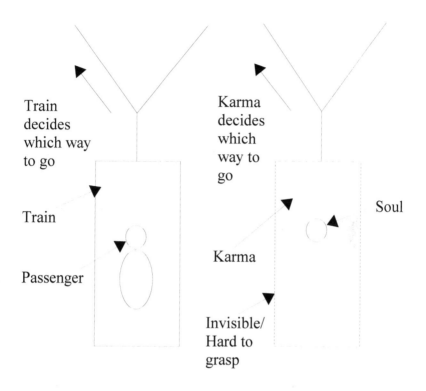

Fig.18

We are just actors acting out the script of Karma. We think we are the doers. But in reality, we are not. Karma is the doer.

If Karma is the doer, how does Karma "do" things through us? How does it micromanage our lives?

Answer: Through the three Material Natures (Gunas): Goodness, Passion and Ignorance.

Hindu Spirituality In A Nutshell

Karma micromanages our lives by manipulating the balance of these three Gunas in our mind at every instant.

Karma is the "doer" through these Gunas (the agents) which are placed in our bodies and intellect.

In this way, we are prisoners of Karma. Karma is the puppeteer and we are puppets in the hands of Karma.

We think we are the doers because Karma is hard to grasp, because it is cannot be perceived by the senses.

Seen in this way, Karma is also referred to as destiny, something which is meant to be. Our fate, as individuals, which has already been written.

There are two aspects to Karma.

- The Account part. Whatever we do gets added to our Karma account and influences our future decisions.
- The Destiny part. What we are going to do has already been decided by our past Karma account.

Seen this way, Karma seems to be an unending cycle. Our past Karma dictates the script of our present decisions, and these decisions in turn add to our future Karma.

Hindu Spirituality In A Nutshell

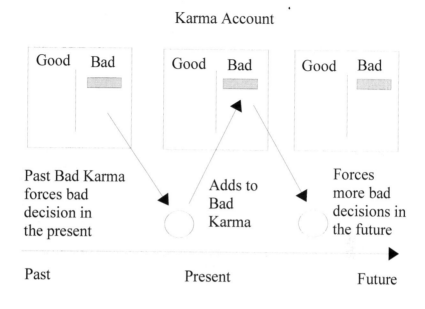

Fig.19

So, in effect, it seems that we can never get rid of our Karma. We are prisoners of our Karma.

Then, how do we break this vicious cycle of Karma which binds us??

Answer: By realizing that what binds us to our Karma is the Maya (illusionary, temporary pleasures) of this Material World.

By renouncing the Maya (illusionary, temporary pleasures) of the Material World.

Hindu Spirituality In A Nutshell

By transcending from the Material World into the Spiritual World.

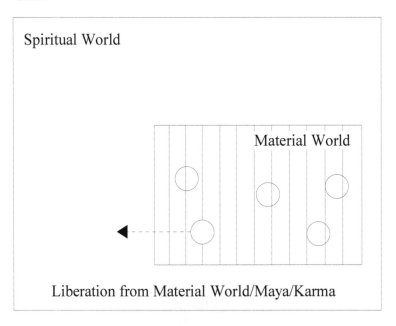

Fig.20

But how do we do that? How do we break out of our Karma? How do we free ourselves from Maya (illusionary, temporary pleasures)? How do we transcend from the Material World and into the Spiritual World?

Answer: By following the various Yoga paths. These Yogic practices have been described in detail in the Bhagavad Gita. We won't discuss these here. Please refer to the many print or online versions of the Bhagavad Gita.

Continuing our discussion, See Fig.21 on the next page.

Hindu Spirituality In A Nutshell

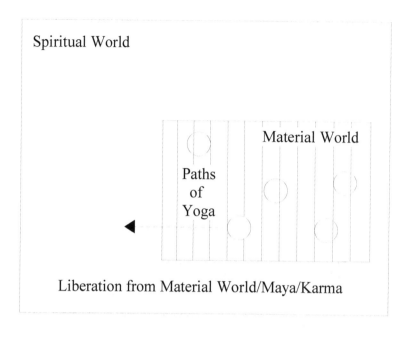

Fig.21

For now, let us just summarize our discussion of Karma in relation to the Material and Spiritual Worlds.

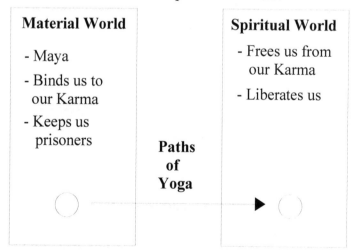

Fig.22

- **Liberation/Mukti**

What does the Soul experience when it gets liberation (also called Mukti / Moksha / Nirvana) from the Material World? What does the Soul experience when it ultimately reaches the Spiritual World?

There are two different beliefs regarding this.

The Dvaita philosophy states this: On reaching the Spiritual World, the Soul keeps it's distinct identity, separate from other Souls and Separate from God.

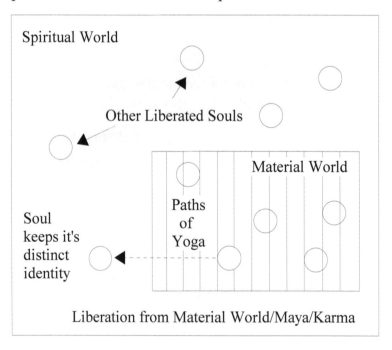

Fig.23

In this stream of belief, the Soul, on entering the Spiritual World can interact with other Souls. This is just like in the Material World where we interact with other people. But with the following essential differences:

In the Material World, the Soul stays in bodies which are mortal and age with time. These bodies are susceptible to diseases, injury, impairment. These bodies die after a lifetime and then the Soul has to assume a new body in rebirth. (The Soul itself is immortal).

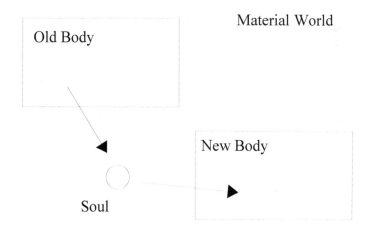

Fig.24

In the Spiritual World the Soul stays in an immortal body, as his own real self. This body never ages with time. It doesn't have diseases, etc like in the Material World. Thus in the Spiritual World, the Soul's body never gets destroyed.

See Fig. 25 on the next page.

Hindu Spirituality In A Nutshell

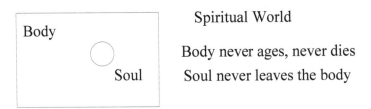

Fig.25

Another difference relates to the quality of life in the Material and Spiritual Worlds.

In the Material World, we undergo suffering in the form of mortality, crime, evil, etc. In the Spiritual World, these Bad things are not present. Instead, in the Spiritual World, the Souls are in their own (ageless) bodies and undertake all kinds of creative and pleasurable activities in beautiful surroundings. It is a place of Supreme Bliss.

In this Dvaita philosophy of Hinduism, God Himself is present in personal forms in the Spiritual World, and the Souls can interact with Him.

On the other hand, the Advaita philosophy states this: When the Soul attains Liberation/Mukti from the Material World, it loses it's own separate identity and merges with God Himself.

Here, God is the infinite, all-pervading, impersonal, consciousness (which is referred to as Brahman).

Hindu Spirituality In A Nutshell

The Spiritual World itself IS God.

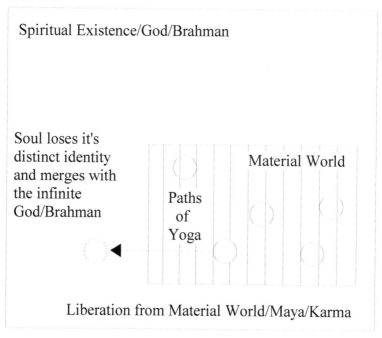

Fig.26

Just like a drop of water loses it's identity in the ocean and it BECOMES the ocean, the Soul loses it's identity in Brahman and BECOMES Brahman and experiences Supreme Bliss.

In Advaita, once in the Spiritual World, as Brahman, the Soul experiences Supreme Bliss characterized by:

- Sat – means Truth, pure and absolute.
- Chit – means Consciousness, pure and absolute.
- Anand – means Bliss, pure and absolute.

Hindu Spirituality In A Nutshell

- **The Journey Home**

All Souls are initially in the Spiritual World.

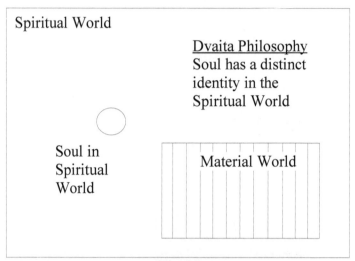

Fig.27

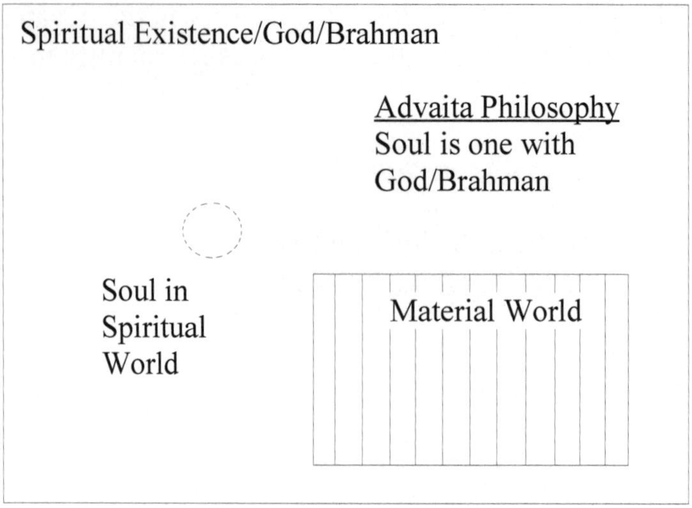

Fig.28

Hindu Spirituality In A Nutshell

But, for some reason or another, some Souls fall into the Material World.

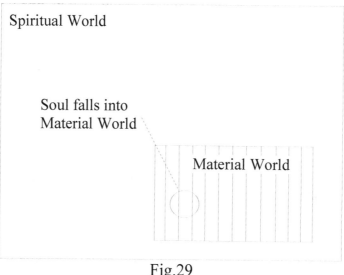

Fig.29

Why the Soul falls into the Material World from the Spiritual World, is explained as follows:

When the Soul is in the Spiritual World initially, the Soul is an enlightened being, knowing the presence of God.

According to Dvaita Philosophy, in the Spiritual World the Soul knows and interacts with God in personal form.

In Advaita philosophy, the Soul is a part of God/Brahman experiencing Sat (Truth), Chit (Consciousness) and Anand (Bliss) in their purest form.

Hindu Spirituality In A Nutshell

In both beliefs, the Soul residing in the Spiritual World accepts God's existence (in personal or impersonal form) and authority.

But at some point of time, false ego suddenly takes over the Soul, causing him to deny the existence/authority of God.

When this happens, the Soul seeks to distance itself from God. It desires to go away from the Spiritual World, and according to it's wishes, falls into the Material World. The Material World is made exactly for such Souls, who want to go away from God.

Once in the Material World, Maya/Karma/false ego takes over and binds the Soul. And he stays here till he acknowledges the existence and authority of God.

How does the Soul do this? How does he acknowledge the existence and authority of God?

By realizing the reality (as described throughout this book) and adopting a Path of Yoga, which frees him from the shackles of Karma and rids him of the false ego.

When this happens, the Soul is liberated, and returns to the Spiritual World.

The Material World is made with so many defects (and

consequently, suffering) in comparison with the Spiritual World because it is meant to be the stick in a carrot-stick policy of God. The carrot is the blissful existence of the Spiritual World.

The two, taken together, serve as inducements for the lost Soul to return to His rightful abode (the Spiritual World) with the realization of God's existence and authority.

Hindu Spirituality In A Nutshell

Printed in Great Britain by
Amazon.co.uk, Ltd.,
Marston Gate.